Time to Bak

by Sonya Hundal
Illustrated by Steliyana Doneva

Contents

OXFORD
UNIVERSITY PRESS

Meet Sonya!

I wash my hands. Then I can start to bake!

Sonya

apron

Sonya is a **baker**.

At the mill

I need **flour** to make bread. I get flour from this old mill.

sail

Hello, I'm the miller.

The miller **grinds** wheat into flour. The flour is put into sacks.

flour

wheat

Make the mix

I put the flour in the bowl. I add **yeast**.
Then I make it wet.

I squash and fold the mix. Then I **mould** the mix into **loaf** shapes.

Then I can pop them in to bake.

Baked!

I tap the bread to check that it is baked.
It has a **hollow** sound if it is baked.

a baked loaf of bread

Success!

basket

I put the bread into paper bags. When my
baskets are full of bags, I can take them to sell.

At the market

I sell my bread at a market. This is my stand.

stand

People like to take a loaf of bread home for their families.

Lots of bread

Some bakers make lots and lots of bread. Their bread is carried in lorries to supermarkets.

Have you tried these sorts of bread?

French stick

breadsticks

pitta

bagel

This is a flat bread called pitta.

Let's clean up

After I have baked my bread, it's time to clean up!

Then it's time for lunch! I like these on my bread.

What would you put on bread?

Look it up!

baker   a person that makes bread and cakes

flour   a fine powder made from corn or wheat

grind   to crush a thing into powder

hollow   when a thing is not solid

loaf   bread that is baked in one bit

mould   if you mould a thing, you make it into a shape

yeast   a fungus that makes bread rise

Index

The *Look it up!* section is also called a Glossary. You can use it to look up the meanings of words that are in **bold** in this book. The Index will help you find key information.